Carbon Capture and Storage: Can It Save the Planet?

Contents

Preface
Introduction
Chapter 1: Introduction to Carbon Capture and Storage
Chapter 2: The Science Behind Carbon Capture and Storage
Chapter 3: Current Technologies and Innovations in CCS
Chapter 4: Major Industries Using or Exploring CCS

Chapter 5: Economic Feasibility of Carbon Capture and Storage
Chapter 6: Challenges and Barriers to CCS Adoption
Chapter 7: Environmental Impact and Potential Benefits of CCS

Chapter 8: Policy and Regulatory Frameworks for CCS
Chapter 9: The Future of Carbon Capture and Storage
Conclusion: Can CCS Save the Planet?
Glossary

Preface

The global effort to mitigate climate change has brought carbon capture and storage (CCS) to the forefront as a potential solution to reduce carbon dioxide (CO_2) emissions. As industries and governments strive to decarbonize, CCS offers the possibility of capturing carbon emissions from industrial processes and safely storing them underground. However, the question remains—can CCS play a significant role in saving the planet from the worst impacts of climate change?

This book, *Carbon Capture and Storage: Can It Save the Planet?*, is part of the Gosships Learning Series, designed to provide a clear understanding of CCS technologies and their potential to contribute to global decarbonization efforts. From foundational knowledge to real-world case studies, this book covers the science, economics, and regulatory frameworks surrounding CCS, as well as the challenges and opportunities it presents.

Whether you are an industry professional or a policymaker, this book offers practical insights and prepares you to engage with carbon capture and storage in a meaningful way. As with all books in the Gosships Learning Series, this resource includes a certification exam to test your comprehension, ensuring that the knowledge gained can be applied in professional settings.

Introduction

Welcome to *Carbon Capture and Storage: Can It Save the Planet?*—a comprehensive guide designed to explore the potential of CCS as a game-changer in the fight against climate change. As part of the Gosships Learning Series, this book aims to bridge the knowledge gap for professionals, providing a detailed look at how CCS technologies can be implemented and scaled across industries.

In this book, we will explore the following key areas:

- **Understanding Carbon Capture**: Gain insights into the science behind capturing carbon emissions and the methods used in various industries.

- **Technologies for Carbon Storage**: Learn about geological and chemical storage solutions that ensure captured carbon is safely sequestered.

- **Economic Considerations**: Explore the costs, benefits, and economic models that support the viability of CCS projects.

- **Regulatory Frameworks**: Understand the policies and regulations governing CCS around the world, including incentives and compliance requirements.

- **Case Studies**: Review real-world examples of CCS in action, highlighting both successes and challenges.

After completing this book, you will have the opportunity to take a certification exam to test your knowledge and understanding of CCS. Upon successful completion, you can obtain a Certificate of Achievement through the Gosships Learning Series platform at www.gosships.com.

Who is this book for?

This book is designed for:

- Environmental professionals seeking to deepen their knowledge of carbon capture and storage technologies.

- Industrial engineers and managers aiming to implement CCS solutions within their operations.

- Students and aspiring environmental scientists looking to gain a foundational understanding of CCS.

- Policymakers and regulatory bodies involved in shaping the future of carbon management and climate mitigation strategies.

By mastering the concepts in this book, you will be well-equipped to navigate the complexities of CCS, contribute to sustainability efforts, and understand the role of carbon capture in addressing the global climate crisis.

Gosships Learning Series 2024/2025

1. Hydrogen: The Fuel of the Future
2. Green Ammonia: The Next Big Thing in Shipping
3. Decarbonizing Shipping: Pathways to Zero Emissions
4. Battery Technology for Industrial Applications
5. Carbon Capture and Storage: Can It Save the Planet?
6. Biofuels 101: Turning Waste into Energy
7. Understanding LNG (Liquefied Natural Gas)
8. Methanol as a Marine Fuel
9. Offshore Wind Energy: The Future of Renewable Power
10. Tidal and Wave Energy: Harnessing the Ocean
11. Electrofuels: The Next Generation of Carbon-Neutral Fuels
12. Energy Storage Systems for Grid Reliability
13. Hydrogen Fuel Cells for Transportation
14. Solar Energy Innovations: Beyond Solar Panels
15. Smart Grids: The Backbone of Future Energy Systems
16. Ammonia-Hydrogen Blends: A Dual Fuel Solution?
17. Nuclear Power: Small Modular Reactors for a Low-Carbon Future
18. Hydropower: The Oldest Renewable Energy Source
19. Decentralized Energy Systems: Microgrids for Resilience
20. Energy Efficiency Technologies for Industry
21. Hydrogen Production from Seawater
22. Fuel Cells for Maritime Applications
23. Geothermal Energy: Unlocking Earth's Heat
24. Future of EV Charging Infrastructure
25. Synthetic Fuels: Bridging the Gap to Decarbonization
26. Cybersecurity for Maritime and Offshore Operations
27. AI and Automation in Shipping and Logistics
28. Digital Twins in Maritime: Revolutionizing Asset Management

29. Risk Management in Offshore and Maritime Operations
30. Compliance with IMO 2020 Regulations
31. Sustainable Ship Design: Reducing Environmental Impact
32. Marine Renewable Energy: Wave, Tidal, and Offshore Wind Integration
33. Ballast Water Management Systems
34. Blockchain Technology in Shipping: Improving Transparency & Efficiency
35. Effective Supply Chain Management for Energy Industries
36. Leadership in the Energy Transition
37. Effective Crisis Management in Maritime Operations
38. Shipyard Safety Management Systems
39. Port State Control (PSC) Inspection Readiness
40. Remote Vessel Operations and Autonomous Shipping
41. Optimizing Fleet Performance with Data Analytics
42. Maritime Environmental Regulations: Staying Ahead of Compliance
43. Advanced Maintenance Strategies: Condition Monitoring & Predictive Maintenance
44. Global LNG Market: Trends and Opportunities
45. Incident Investigation in Maritime Operations
46. International Maritime Law: Key Concepts and Applications
47. Emergency Preparedness and Response for Offshore Oil & Gas
48. Energy Transition Strategies for Oil and Gas Companies
49. Maritime Drones: Applications and Safety Considerations
50. Effective Project Management in Offshore Energy Projects

All Rights Reserved Disclaimer

The contents of this book, including but not limited to all text, graphics, images, logos, and designs, are the intellectual property of Gosships LLC and are protected by copyright law. No part of this publication may be reproduced, distributed, transmitted, displayed, or modified in any form or by any means, including photocopying, recording, or other electronic or mechanical methods, without the prior written permission of the publisher, except in the case of brief quotations in critical reviews or articles.

The information contained within this book is for educational purposes only and is provided "as is" without warranty of any kind, either expressed or implied. The authors and publishers disclaim any liability for any direct, indirect, or consequential loss or damage arising from the use of the material in this book.

For permissions or inquiries, please contact: admin@gosships.com

© 2024 Gosships LLC. All rights reserved.

Chapter 1

Introduction to Carbon Capture and Storage

Climate change has become one of the most pressing global challenges of our time, driven largely by the rapid increase in greenhouse gas emissions from human activities. Carbon dioxide (CO_2), one of the primary greenhouse gases, is responsible for much of the warming we've experienced over the past century. To mitigate climate change, we need to reduce our CO_2 emissions dramatically.

One of the emerging solutions to this problem is **Carbon Capture and Storage (CCS)**. CCS is a technology that captures carbon dioxide from industrial processes or directly from the air and stores it underground to prevent it from entering the atmosphere. In theory, CCS could help reduce emissions from the energy, industrial, and transportation sectors, which are some of the biggest contributors to global CO_2 emissions.

The big question is: **Can CCS really save the planet?** In this book, we will explore the potential of CCS as a climate solution, examine the technology behind it, discuss the industries that are exploring its use, and look at the economic and environmental factors that influence its feasibility.

Chapter 2

The Science Behind Carbon Capture and Storage

Carbon Capture and Storage is a multi-step process that involves capturing CO_2 at its source, transporting it to a storage site, and storing it underground in deep geological formations. Let's break down each step.

Capturing Carbon

There are three main types of carbon capture:

- **Post-combustion capture**: In this method, CO_2 is captured after the fossil fuel has been burned. This is the most commonly used method and can be applied to existing power plants and industrial facilities.
- **Pre-combustion capture**: This involves converting fossil fuels into a mixture of hydrogen and CO_2 before combustion. The CO_2 is captured before the fuel is burned, and the hydrogen can be used as a clean energy source.
- **Oxy-fuel combustion**: This method burns fossil fuels in oxygen rather than air, resulting in a concentrated stream of CO_2 that is easier to capture.

Transporting Carbon

Once captured, CO_2 needs to be transported to a storage site, which is typically done through pipelines. CO_2 can also be transported by ships or trucks, though pipelines are the most efficient method for large-scale operations.

Storing Carbon

The final step is to store the captured CO_2 deep underground in geological formations, such as depleted oil and gas fields or saline aquifers. These underground storage sites are carefully selected to ensure that the CO_2 will remain trapped and not leak into the atmosphere. Monitoring systems are put in place to ensure the long-term safety of the storage.

CCS differs from natural carbon sequestration methods like planting trees, as it involves human-engineered processes designed to store large amounts of CO_2 quickly and efficiently. While natural solutions are crucial, CCS can capture emissions from industrial sources that are hard to eliminate through other means.

Chapter 3

Current Technologies and Innovations in CCS

Several technologies are already being used to capture carbon, with varying degrees of efficiency and cost. Here's an overview of the main CCS technologies in use today:

Post-Combustion Capture

This is the most widely deployed CCS technology, especially in power plants. In post-combustion capture, CO_2 is separated from the flue gases after combustion. Technologies like **amine-based chemical absorption** are commonly used to absorb the CO_2. After absorption, the CO_2 is separated from the solvent, compressed, and transported for storage.

Pre-Combustion Capture

Pre-combustion capture is mostly used in industries like hydrogen production and gasification plants. The fuel is converted into a mixture of hydrogen and CO_2 before combustion, allowing the CO_2 to be captured more efficiently.

Direct Air Capture (DAC)

A promising innovation in CCS is **Direct Air Capture (DAC)**, which captures CO_2 directly from the air rather than from industrial emissions. Although DAC technology is still expensive and energy-intensive, it has the potential to capture carbon at a global scale, including CO_2 that has already been emitted into the atmosphere.

Carbon Utilization

In addition to storing CO_2, some companies are exploring ways to use it. **Carbon utilization** involves turning captured CO_2 into valuable products like fuels, chemicals, and building materials. While this doesn't solve the problem of CO_2 emissions completely, it can offset some of the costs of CCS and reduce the demand for virgin resources.

As the need for CCS grows, so does innovation. Researchers are constantly working on new ways to improve the efficiency and affordability of CCS technologies, such as using materials like **metal-organic frameworks (MOFs)** to enhance CO_2 capture or exploring biological approaches to capture carbon through algae.

Chapter 4
Major Industries Using or Exploring CCS

Several industries are looking into CCS as a way to reduce their carbon footprint. These sectors are typically heavy emitters, and CCS offers a solution for cutting emissions without completely overhauling their operations.

Power Generation

Power plants that burn fossil fuels, particularly coal and natural gas, are major contributors to CO_2 emissions. CCS allows these plants to continue operating while significantly reducing their emissions. **Bioenergy with Carbon Capture and Storage (BECCS)** is another approach in which bioenergy is combined with CCS to create a system that not only captures CO_2 but also removes it from the atmosphere.

Cement and Steel Production

The cement and steel industries are among the hardest to decarbonize because their manufacturing processes release large amounts of CO_2. Cement production, in particular, emits CO_2 as a byproduct of limestone calcination. CCS offers a way to capture emissions directly from these processes, making it a critical technology for decarbonizing heavy industry.

Oil and Gas

The oil and gas industry has been using CCS for years as part of **Enhanced Oil Recovery (EOR)**, where CO_2 is injected into oil reservoirs to increase oil production. While this increases fossil fuel extraction, it also provides an opportunity to store CO_2 permanently underground. The oil and gas sector is now looking into using CCS to reduce emissions from refining and petrochemical processes.

Case Studies

Several projects around the world are already demonstrating the feasibility of CCS. For example, the **Boundary Dam Power Station** in Canada was the world's first large-scale CCS project at a coal-fired power plant, capturing over 1 million tons of CO_2 per year. The **Sleipner Field** in Norway has been injecting CO_2 into geological formations since 1996, storing millions of tons of CO_2.

Chapter 5

Economic Feasibility of Carbon Capture and Storage

CCS technologies, while promising, are not cheap. The costs of capturing, transporting, and storing CO_2 are significant, and this has been a major barrier to widespread adoption. However, the economics of CCS are slowly improving as the technology advances.

Costs of CCS

Capturing CO_2 is the most expensive part of the CCS process, accounting for about 70-80% of the total cost. Transporting CO_2 through pipelines or ships also adds to the cost, especially if the storage site is far from the source. Finally, developing secure storage sites and ensuring long-term monitoring require significant investment.

Government Incentives

To make CCS more economically viable, governments are offering subsidies and tax credits. For example, in the United States, the **45Q tax credit** provides financial incentives for companies that capture and store CO_2. Similar programs exist in the European Union and other regions, aiming to lower the cost barriers and promote CCS adoption.

Carbon Pricing

Another key factor in the economics of CCS is **carbon pricing**. By putting a price on carbon emissions through mechanisms like carbon taxes or emissions trading systems, governments create a financial incentive for companies to invest in CCS. The higher the price of emitting CO_2, the more attractive CCS becomes as a solution.

Carbon Utilization

In some cases, companies can offset the costs of CCS by turning captured CO_2 into valuable products. This practice, known as **carbon utilization**, offers a potential revenue stream that can help finance CCS projects. For example, captured CO_2 can be used to produce synthetic fuels, chemicals, or building materials.

Chapter 6

Challenges and Barriers to CCS Adoption

Despite its potential, CCS faces several significant challenges that limit its widespread use.

Technological Challenges

Capturing CO_2 efficiently remains a major technological hurdle. Current capture technologies are energy-intensive, requiring a lot of energy to separate CO_2 from flue gases. This can offset some of the emissions reductions achieved through CCS. Developing more energy-efficient capture technologies is essential for CCS to reach its full potential.

Infrastructure Needs

CCS requires a robust infrastructure for transporting CO_2 from capture sites to storage locations. This means building extensive networks of pipelines or developing alternative transportation methods, such as shipping CO_2. Developing this infrastructure on a global scale is both costly and logistically challenging.

Environmental and Safety Concerns

One of the biggest concerns surrounding CCS is the risk of CO_2 leakage from underground storage sites. While geological formations are carefully selected to minimize this risk, monitoring systems must be in place to ensure the CO_2 remains securely stored for decades or even centuries. Public perception of these risks can also lead to opposition from communities near proposed storage sites.

Social Acceptance

In some cases, CCS projects face opposition from local communities, either due to environmental concerns or a lack of understanding about the technology. Building public trust and educating people about the benefits and safety of CCS is key to its broader adoption.

Chapter 7

Environmental Impact and Potential Benefits of CCS

The primary benefit of CCS is its potential to significantly reduce CO_2 emissions, particularly from sectors that are difficult to decarbonize. By capturing and storing emissions that would otherwise be released into the atmosphere, CCS could help the world meet its climate goals.

Meeting Climate Goals

According to the Intergovernmental Panel on Climate Change (IPCC), limiting global temperature rise to 1.5°C will require not only reducing emissions but also removing CO_2 from the atmosphere. CCS can play a critical role in achieving this by capturing emissions from power plants, industrial processes, and even directly from the air.

Reducing Emissions from Hard-to-Abate Sectors

Sectors like cement, steel, and chemical production are difficult to decarbonize due to the nature of their processes. CCS provides one of the few options for reducing emissions from these industries without completely changing their operations.

Complementing Renewable Energy

While renewable energy is essential for reducing emissions, it cannot solve the climate crisis on its own. CCS can complement renewable energy by capturing emissions from fossil fuel plants during the transition to a fully renewable energy system. Additionally, CCS can be combined with bioenergy (BECCS) to create a system that actively removes CO_2 from the atmosphere.

Chapter 8
Policy and Regulatory Frameworks for CCS

Governments play a crucial role in supporting the development and deployment of CCS. Without the right policies and regulations, it will be difficult for CCS to scale up to the level needed to make a meaningful impact.

Existing Policies

Several countries have already introduced policies to support CCS. In the United States, the 45Q tax credit provides financial incentives for companies that capture and store CO_2. In the European Union, CCS is part of the **EU Emissions Trading System (ETS)**, which puts a price on carbon and encourages industries to reduce their emissions.

International Collaboration

CCS is a global challenge, and international cooperation is essential for its success. Organizations like the **Global CCS Institute** and the **Carbon Capture and Storage Association** are working to promote CCS research, share best practices, and encourage investment in CCS projects.

The Need for Strong Regulations

To ensure the long-term safety and effectiveness of CCS, governments need to establish clear regulations for CO_2 storage. These regulations should include guidelines for site selection, monitoring, and reporting, as well as liability for any potential CO_2 leakage.

Chapter 9

The Future of Carbon Capture and Storage

As the world moves toward a low-carbon future, CCS will likely play a key role in reducing emissions from sectors that are hard to decarbonize. However, several factors will determine the future success of CCS.

Scaling CCS Globally

To have a significant impact on global emissions, CCS needs to be scaled up dramatically. This will require major investments in infrastructure, research, and development, as well as international cooperation.

Integrating CCS with Renewable Energy

As renewable energy sources like solar and wind continue to grow, CCS can serve as a bridge technology, helping to reduce emissions from fossil fuel plants during the transition to a cleaner energy system. Additionally, combining CCS with bioenergy (BECCS) offers the potential for negative emissions, actively removing CO_2 from the atmosphere.

New Business Models for CCS

For CCS to become economically viable on a large scale, new business models are needed. These could include carbon pricing mechanisms, carbon utilization opportunities, and public-private partnerships. The question of who will bear the costs of CCS—governments, industries, or consumers—will also need to be addressed.

Chapter 10

Conclusion: Can CCS Save the Planet?

Carbon Capture and Storage is a powerful tool in the fight against climate change, but it is not a silver bullet. CCS can significantly reduce emissions from key industries and power plants, but it must be combined with other solutions, such as renewable energy, energy efficiency, and natural carbon sequestration, to achieve global climate goals.

While CCS has the potential to play a critical role in decarbonizing the world's economy, it faces technological, economic, and social challenges that must be addressed for it to be widely adopted. Governments, industries, and researchers must work together to overcome these barriers and scale up CCS to the levels needed to make a meaningful impact on global emissions.

In the end, CCS is not about saving the planet on its own but about contributing to a larger portfolio of solutions that can collectively mitigate the worst effects of climate change. If deployed correctly, it can be an essential part of the strategy to create a sustainable, low-carbon future for generations to come.

Glossary - Carbon Capture and Storage: Can It Save the Planet?

1. **Anthropogenic CO_2**: Carbon dioxide (CO_2) emissions resulting from human activities such as fossil fuel combustion and industrial processes.

2. **BECCS (Bioenergy with Carbon Capture and Storage)**: A technology that combines bioenergy production with carbon capture to achieve negative emissions.

3. **Bicarbonate**: A form of carbon found in ocean storage as part of the carbon capture and storage process, helping to neutralize CO_2.

4. **Biomass**: Organic materials (e.g., wood, crops) used in energy production, often coupled with CCS to reduce net carbon emissions.

5. **Caprock**: A dense, impermeable layer of rock that acts as a seal, preventing stored CO_2 from escaping in geological storage.

6. **Carbon Accounting**: The process of measuring and tracking carbon emissions, removals, and offsets in industries or governments.

7. **Carbon Capture**: The process of trapping carbon dioxide (CO_2) at its emission source, such as power plants or industrial facilities, to prevent it from entering the atmosphere.

8. **Carbon Dioxide (CO_2)**: A greenhouse gas responsible for climate change, commonly emitted through the burning of fossil fuels.

9. **Carbon Intensity**: The amount of CO_2 emissions produced per unit of energy or output, used as a metric for industries aiming to reduce their carbon footprint.

10. **Carbon Neutrality**: Achieving a balance between emitting carbon and absorbing carbon through offsetting or carbon capture methods.

11. **Carbon Sink**: A natural or artificial reservoir that absorbs more CO_2 from the atmosphere than it releases, such as forests or oceans.

12. **CCS (Carbon Capture and Storage)**: A technology designed to capture carbon dioxide emissions and store them underground or in other secure locations.

13. **CCUS (Carbon Capture, Utilization, and Storage)**: Similar to CCS but includes the utilization of captured carbon dioxide for other industrial purposes.

14. **Chemical Absorption**: A process used in carbon capture where chemical solvents absorb CO_2 from flue gases at industrial sites.

15. **Climeworks**: A company that focuses on direct air capture (DAC) technology to remove CO_2 directly from the atmosphere.

16. **CO_2-EOR (CO_2 Enhanced Oil Recovery)**: A process that injects captured CO_2 into oil reservoirs to boost oil production while storing the CO_2 underground.

17. **CO_2 Pipeline**: Infrastructure used to transport captured carbon dioxide from its emission source to a storage site.

18. **CO_2 Sequestration**: The long-term storage of carbon dioxide in geological formations, the ocean, or other reservoirs to prevent its release into the atmosphere.

19. **DAC (Direct Air Capture)**: A technology that captures carbon dioxide directly from the air, removing existing atmospheric CO_2.

20. **Decarbonization**: The process of reducing carbon dioxide emissions from industrial activities, energy production, and other sectors.

21. **Deep Saline Aquifers**: Underground layers of porous rock filled with salty water, used as storage sites for captured CO_2 in geological sequestration.

22. **EOR (Enhanced Oil Recovery)**: The process of injecting gases or liquids, including CO_2, into oil reservoirs to increase oil extraction and store CO_2.

23. **Flue Gas**: Exhaust gases emitted from industrial processes, which contain CO_2 and other pollutants that can be captured.

24. **Geological Sequestration**: The storage of captured CO_2 in underground rock formations, such as depleted oil fields or deep saline aquifers.

25. **GHG (Greenhouse Gases)**: Gases, including CO_2, methane, and nitrous oxide, that trap heat in the atmosphere and contribute to global warming.

26. **Greenhouse Effect**: The warming of Earth's surface caused by greenhouse gases trapping heat from the sun in the atmosphere.

27. **Hydrated Lime ($Ca(OH)_2$)**: A chemical used in certain carbon capture processes to absorb CO_2 from industrial emissions.

28. **Injection Well**: A well drilled to inject captured CO_2 deep into underground geological formations for storage.

29. **IPCC (Intergovernmental Panel on Climate Change)**: A United Nations body that provides scientific assessments on climate change, including recommendations on CCS.

30. **Leakage**: The unintended escape of stored CO_2 from its storage site, a critical risk that CCS technologies aim to mitigate.

31. **Liquid Solvents**: Chemicals used in carbon capture processes to absorb CO_2 from emissions before the CO_2 is separated and stored.

32. **Membrane Separation**: A technology that uses selective membranes to separate CO_2 from other gases in emissions streams.

33. **Methane (CH_4)**: A potent greenhouse gas often emitted from industrial processes and landfills, contributing to climate change.

34. **Mitigation**: Actions taken to reduce or prevent the emission of greenhouse gases, including through technologies like CCS.

35. **Negative Emissions**: The removal of more carbon dioxide from the atmosphere than is emitted, often achieved through BECCS or DAC technologies.

36. **Ocean Sequestration**: The process of storing captured CO_2 in the deep ocean, where it dissolves into the water and forms carbon compounds.

37. **Offsets**: Actions taken to compensate for CO_2 emissions, such as investing in carbon capture or reforestation projects.

38. **Oxyfuel Combustion**: A carbon capture process that burns fuel in oxygen rather than air to produce a concentrated CO_2 stream for easier capture.

39. **Paris Agreement**: A global accord that sets targets for reducing greenhouse gas emissions to limit global temperature rise.

40. **Permeability**: The ability of rock formations to allow fluids or gases, such as CO_2, to pass through, important for geological sequestration sites.

41. **Post-Combustion Capture**: A method of capturing CO_2 after fossil fuels have been burned, typically using solvents to remove CO_2 from flue gases.

42. **Pre-Combustion Capture**: The process of capturing CO_2 before fossil fuels are burned, often through gasification, producing a concentrated CO_2 stream.

43. **Reservoir**: A geological formation, such as a deep saline aquifer or depleted oil field, used to store captured CO_2.

44. **Saturation**: The point at which a storage site, like an underground reservoir, can no longer hold additional CO_2.

45. **Sequestration**: The process of capturing and storing CO_2 for the long term to prevent its release into the atmosphere.

46. **Supercritical CO_2**: CO_2 that is held at high pressure and temperature, where it exhibits both liquid and gas properties, making it ideal for underground injection.

47. **Sustainability**: Practices that ensure natural resources and the environment are protected and maintained for future generations, often associated with carbon capture efforts.

48. **Thermal Oxidation**: A carbon capture process where high temperatures are used to convert organic compounds into CO_2 for capture.

49. **Utilization**: The process of using captured CO_2 for industrial purposes, such as in building materials or enhanced oil recovery.

50. **Zero Emissions**: The goal of reducing carbon dioxide emissions to zero, either through eliminating emissions or offsetting them via CCS and other methods.